WHAT KIND OF SPENDER ARE YOU?

By Brooke Rowe

45th
Parallel
Press

Published in the United States of America by Cherry Lake Publishing
Ann Arbor, Michigan
www.cherrylakepublishing.com

Reading Adviser: Marla Conn, ReadAbility, Inc.
Book Designer: Melinda Millward

Photo Credits: © William Perugini/Shutterstock.com, back cover, 4; © monkeybusinessimages/Thinkstock.com, back cover, 4; © Bananastock/Thinkstock Images, cover, 1; © Brent Hofacker/Shutterstock Images, 6; © MSPhotographic/Shutterstock Images, 6;© Lisovskaya Natalia/Shutterstock Images, 7; © WilliamEdwards14/Shutterstock Images, 7; © Ra'id Khalil/Shutterstock Images, 8; © dezi/Shutterstock Images, 8; © Anton_Invanov/Shutterstock Images, 9; © Dobo Kristian/Shutterstock Images, 9; © DragonImages/Deposit Photos, 10; © Lewis Tse Pui Lung/Shutterstock Images, 10; © Goodluz/Shutterstock Images, 11; © R.legosyn/Shutterstock Images, 11; © sasasasa/iStockphoto, 12, 30; © wavebreakmedia/Shutterstock Images, 12; © Jupiterimages/Thinkstock Images, 13; © sUs_angel/Shutterstock Images, 13; © iofoto/Shutterstock Images, 14; © Monkey Business Images/Shutterstock Images, 14; © FXQuadro/Shutterstock Images, 15, 31; © Michael Shake/Shutterstock Images, 15; © arek_malang/Shutterstock Images, 16; © Stanisic Vladimir/Shutterstock Images, 16; © Oris Arisara/Shutterstock Images, 17; © GSerban/Shutterstock Images, 18; © CREA-TISTA/Thinkstock Images, 18; © savageultralight/Shutterstock Images, 19; © Neil Lockhart/Shutterstock Images, 19; © dean bertoncelj/Shutterstock Images, 20, 30; © karamysh/Shutterstock Images, 20; © Doremi/Shutterstock Images, 21; © Syda Productions/Shutterstock Images, 21; © June Marie Sobrito/Shutterstock Images, 22; © gpointstudio/Shutterstock Images, 22; © Champion studio/Shutterstock Images, 23; © MNStudio/Shutterstock Images, 23; © Sylvie Bouchard/Shutterstock Images, 24; © 06photo / Shutterstock.com, 24; © ckeyes888/Shutterstock Images, 25; © George Dolgikh/Shutterstock Images, 25; © BONNIN-STUDIO/Shutterstock Images, 26; © r.nagy / Shutterstock.com, 26; © melis/Shutterstock Images, 27; © Alena Stalmashonak/Shutterstock Images, 27; © Stephen Coburn/Shutterstock Images, 28; © Kris Schmidt/Shutterstock Images, 28; © Rasulov/Shutterstock Images, 29; © Kseniia Perminova/Shutterstock Images, 29; © Pressmaster/Shutterstock Images, 31

Graphic Element Credits: © Silhouette Lover/Shutterstock Images, back cover, multiple interior pages; © Arevik/Shutterstock Images, back cover, multiple interior pages; © tukkki/Shutterstock Images, multiple interior pages; © paprika/Shutterstock Images, 24

45th Parallel Press is an imprint of Cherry Lake Publishing.

Library of Congress Cataloging-in-Publication Data

Rowe, Brooke.
    What kind of spender are you? / Brooke Rowe.
pages cm. — (Best quiz ever)
Includes index.
ISBN 978-1-63470-040-5 (hardcover) — ISBN 978-1-63470-094-8 (pdf) —
ISBN 978-1-63470-067-2 (pbk.) — ISBN 978-1-63470-121-1 (ebook)
1. Money—Miscellanea—Juvenile literature. 2. Personality tests—Juvenile literature. I. Title.

HG221.5.R69 2016
332.024—dc23   2015009917

Printed in the United States of America
Corporate Graphics

Table of Contents

Introduction

Hey! Welcome to the Best Quiz Ever series. This is a book. Duh. But it's also a pretty awesome quiz. Don't worry. It's not about math. Or history. Or anything you might get graded on. Snooze.

This is a quiz all about YOU.

To Take the Best Quiz Ever:

Answer honestly!
Keep track of your answers. But don't write in the book!
(Hint: Make a copy of this handy chart.)
Don't see the answer you want? Pick the closest one.
Take it alone. Take it with friends!
Have fun! Obviously.

Question 1 _____   Question 7 _____

Question 2 _____   Question 8 _____

Question 3 _____   Question 9 _____

Question 4 _____   Question 10 _____

Question 5 _____   Question 11 _____

Question 6 _____   Question 12 _____

To get a copy of this activity, visit
www.cherrylakepublishing.com/activities.

You go to breakfast with your friend. What do you order?

A. A piece of toast and water

B. Super Crazy Deluxe **omelet**

C. Sunday Morning Special. Plus one for my friend.

D. Scrambled eggs. Bacon. Coffee cake. More bacon.

Did you know?

In the United States, 70 percent of all bacon is eaten at breakfast time.

If your bank account were an animal, what would it be?

A. A horse

B. A hummingbird

C. A penguin

D. A dead spider

Did you know?

*There are more than 300 **species** of hummingbirds.*

Which of these songs describes you best?

A. "You Can't Always Get What You Want"

B. "Material Girl"

C. "You've Got a
Friend in Me"

D. "If I Had $1,000,000"

Did you know?
iTunes sells more than 21 million
songs every day.

What's in your wallet?

A. The $20 I got for my birthday months ago

B. $10 and rewards cards for local stores

C. $5 and photos
of my friends

D. Pennies, **receipts,**
and empty air

Did you know?
The **U.S. Mint** has been releasing quarters
with different designs for each state since 1999,
and it plans to do so through 2021.

You ask for a ride to the mall. What does your dad say?

A. "Wow, there's a first time for everything!"

B. "Not again! Ask your brother."

C. "Good idea! We need a gift for your sister."

D. "Fine, but you have a $5 limit."

Did you know?
Three of the world's ten largest malls are in Kuala Lumpur, Malaysia.

What's your favorite part of school?

A. Learning important things

B. Dressing up before I catch the bus

C. Meeting so many new people

D. After-school clubs and sports

Did you know?
Skola (sku-LAH) means
school in Swedish.

17

What does your mom say when you ask to go grocery shopping with her?

A. "Sure! You always find the best deals!"

B. "Okay, but no early allowance!"

18

C. "Sure! Let's get donuts on the way."

D. "Okay. But only if you wear a blindfold."

Did you know?
The first Friday in June each year
is National Donut Day.

What scares you about growing up?

A. Spending my life savings on a house

B. Not having time to shop

C. Missing my friends' birthday parties

D. Being responsible for my family's money

Did you know?

A **mansion** in Connecticut costs $190 million, and includes seven bathrooms and a mile of a beach.

Which would be the best place for you to win a gift card for?

A. The outlet mall

B. The coolest store in town

C. A local restaurant

D. Just cash is great.
Thanks!

Did you know?
Each year, shoppers fail to spend more
than $1 billion in gift cards.

You're assigned a book for a school project. How do you get a copy?

A. Check one out for free at the library

B. Buy a hardcover

C. Buy used copies for me and my partner

D. Order one online. Plus some other stuff.

Did you know?
The longest novel ever written is In Search of Lost Time *by Marcel Proust. It is 3,031 pages long.*

What's in your Internet search history?

A. Coupon web sites

B. Fashion blogs

C. My friends' photos

D. Cat videos

Did you know?
YouTube hosts about 2 billion cat videos.

QUESTION 12

While you're walking to school, a bird poops on you. What do you do?

A. Change into the extra shirt in my locker

B. Run toward my favorite store

C. Borrow a friend's sweatshirt

D. Wash it out, obviously!

Did you know?
Some people say that a bird pooping on you brings good luck.

You're done! Now you tally your score. Add up your As, Bs, Cs, and Ds. What letter do you have the most of? BTW, if you have a tie, you're a little bit of both.

As: Saver

You should be a superhero. All you do is save, save, save. Three dollars here, 25 cents there—it adds up! You're smart. You know your money might run off and leave you like a puppy at the dog park. So you keep it on a tight leash. But one benefit to saving cash is that you have money when you need it. So treat yourself once in a while.

Bs: Shop Till You Drop

Look at you go! You have great muscles from carrying those bags. If there's a sale, you're there. Shopping can be a lot of fun. That is, as long as you use what you buy. And you still set some money aside. Just try to set a limit before you head to the mall. And hold on to your receipts. You might change your mind on that neon green dress.

Cs: Share the Wealth

You like to spend. But mostly on other people. You love surprising friends with gifts. You also love to help those in need. You will dump everything from your pockets into a charity bucket. Even if you're on your way to buy something. Generosity is a great quality. But you have to have money before you can give it away. And be careful about giving unexpected gifts. Friends might feel weird not having a gift for you.

Ds: Impulse Buyer

The racks near the checkout were made for people like you. Magazines, gum, key chains—doesn't matter. If it looks cool and you have enough change, you buy it. Check yourself before you wreck yourself! Do you really need that mini bag of chips? Mom already has a giant bag at home. Next time you go shopping, make a list. And stick to it!

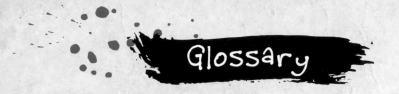

Glossary

mansion (MAN-shuhn) a very large and impressive house

omelet (AHM-lit) beaten eggs that have been cooked in a pan, filled with cheese, vegetables, or meat, and folded over

receipts (ri-SEETZ) pieces of paper showing that money, goods, or services have been received

species (SPEE-seez) groups into which animals and plants of the same type are divided

U.S. Mint (you ess MINT) government factories in the United States that produce coins

Index